American Moments

ABDO
Daughters

THE TRANSCONTINENTAL
RAILROAD

By Alan Pierce

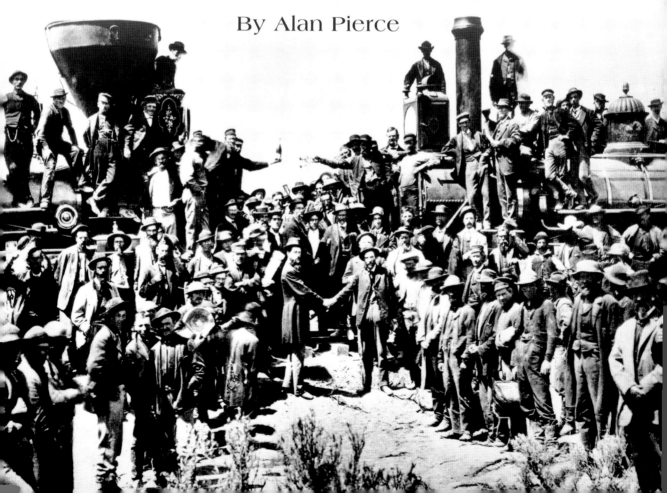

VISIT US AT
WWW.ABDOPUB.COM

Published by ABDO Publishing Company, 4940 Viking Drive, Suite 622, Edina, Minnesota 55435. Copyright © 2005 by Abdo Consulting Group, Inc. International copyrights reserved in all countries. No part of this book may be reproduced in any form without written permission from the publisher. ABDO & Daughters™ is a trademark and logo of ABDO Publishing Company.

Printed in the United States.

Edited by: Melanie A. Howard
Interior Production and Design: Terry Dunham Incorporated
Cover Design: Mighty Media
Photos: Corbis, Library of Congress, Union Pacific Historical Collection

Library of Congress Cataloging-in-Publication Data

Pierce, Alan, 1966-
   The transcontinental railroad / Alan Pierce.
     p. cm. -- (American moments)
   ISBN 1-59197-941-2
   1. Pacific railroads--Juvenile literature. [1. Railroads--History--Juvenile literature.] I. Title. II. Series.

TF25.P23P54 2005
385'.0978--dc22

                                    2004066002

CONTENTS

THE GOLDEN SPIKE

Near the Great Salt Lake, railroad officials and their crews gathered at Promontory Summit in the Utah Territory. On May 10, 1869, they met to celebrate the completion of the United States's only transcontinental railroad. For decades, people had dreamed of a railroad that would connect the country's east and west coasts. Now that formidable task was almost complete.

Gangs of workers had toiled for six years to link Sacramento, California, and Omaha, Nebraska, by rail. The track spanned 1,776 miles (2,858 km) through some of the most challenging terrain in the country. The crews that built the railroad faced the harshness of deserts. They worked in the soaring heights of the Rocky Mountains and Sierra Nevada. All of these obstacles were surmounted by the railroad workers.

Two railroad companies built the transcontinental railroad. The Central Pacific Railroad Company began in Sacramento and advanced eastward. The Union Pacific Railroad started in Omaha and progressed west. Promontory Summit was 690 miles (1,110 km) from Sacramento and 1,086 miles (1,748 km) from Omaha. U.S. railroads had already extended from the east coast to the Missouri River where Omaha was located.

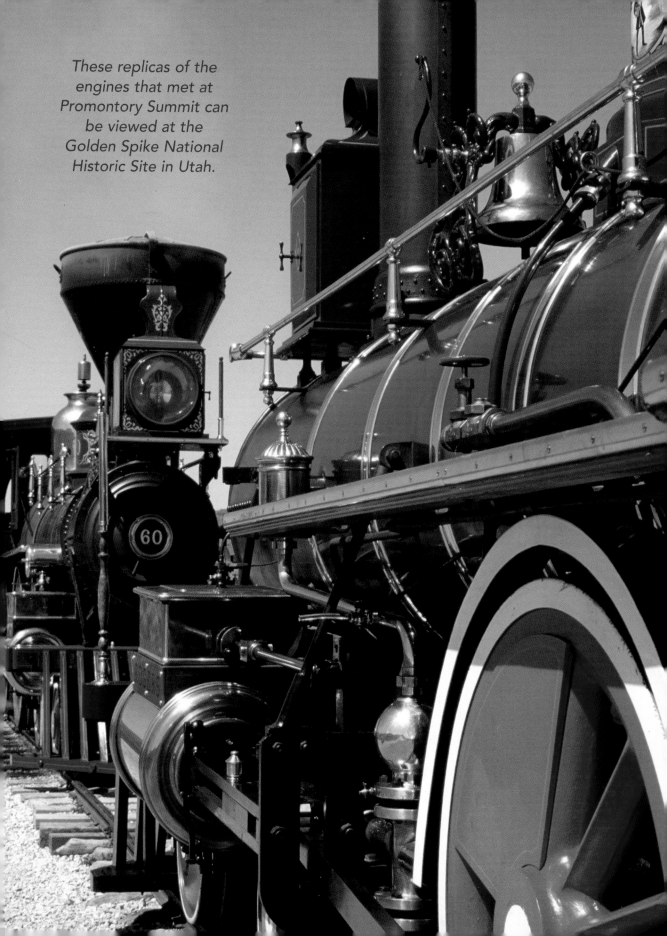

These replicas of the engines that met at Promontory Summit can be viewed at the Golden Spike National Historic Site in Utah.

At Promontory Summit, special spikes were used to mark the final construction. One spike was silver and another was made of gold, silver, and iron. But the most famous spike was the Golden Spike, which was made of 18 ounces (510 g) of gold. A jewelry company in California had engraved words on the spike. Part of the engraving read, "May God continue the unity of our Country as the Railroad unites the two great Oceans of the world."

Central Pacific president Leland Stanford had the honor of tapping the Golden Spike into a hole. But it was another spike that played a key role in the ceremony. A telegraph wire was coiled around an ordinary iron spike. Another telegraph wire was wrapped around Stanford's hammer. When he struck the iron spike, telegraph operators would alert the nation that the transcontinental railroad was finished.

According to some later accounts, Stanford missed the spike and hit the rail. But at the time, no one reported that he had missed the spike. In any case, telegraph operators notified cities throughout the country that the railroad bridged the nation.

The telegraph message set off a wave of celebrations across the United States. Cannons fired in New York City, New York, and in San Francisco, California. Bells tolled in churches and in Independence Hall in Philadelphia, Pennsylvania. In Chicago, Illinois, people turned out to watch a parade seven miles (11 km) long.

These celebrations honored an astonishing achievement. The transcontinental railroad had conquered vast distances and rugged terrain. Thanks to the transcontinental railroad, Americans were much closer than ever.

Leland Stanford

AMERICA EXPANDS WEST

Only 40 years before the transcontinental railroad, the United States had almost no railroad tracks and very few locomotives. In August 1829, the Stourbridge Lion became the first locomotive to run in the United States. The locomotive made a short test run near Honesdale, Pennsylvania. Afterwards, Americans rapidly increased the miles of track in the country. By 1840, about 2,800 miles (4,500 km) of track had been built.

As Americans built more track, they also improved the designs of trains. Locomotives became larger and more powerful. In the 1830s, engineer John Jervis developed the four-wheel swiveling trucks. This apparatus made trains more stable as they rounded curves. One benefit was that trains could travel faster. Another bonus was that engineers could build switchback tracks that zigzagged up steep slopes. This track design allowed trains to climb mountains.

As soon as the railroad appeared in the United States, some people proposed building long lines. A man named William Redfield offered one idea in a pamphlet he published in 1830. Redfield called for building a railroad line from the Atlantic coast to the Mississippi River valley. This line could then be extended to the Pacific Ocean. At the time, the United States claimed the

This picture shows one artist's idea of Manifest Destiny.

Pacific Northwest, but few Americans had settled in this area. California and much of the present-day western United States belonged to Mexico.

Many Americans wanted to expand the size of the country. This ambition was driven by a belief known as Manifest Destiny. The idea of Manifest Destiny maintained that God had sanctioned the United States to expand across North America. Manifest Destiny also assumed that U.S. culture and government were superior to those of other people.

Manifest Destiny prompted the expansion of the United States. One major acquisition was the Republic of Texas, which had been part of Mexico. In 1836, Texas broke away from Mexico and quickly asked to join the United States. Despite the influence of Manifest Destiny, some Americans did not want to admit Texas. Texas permitted slavery, and many Americans in Northern states opposed slavery. Nevertheless, Congress agreed to annex Texas. In 1845, Texas became the twenty-eighth state.

The Mexican government was offended when Texas joined the United States. Mexicans still considered Texas to be part of their country. Relations between Mexico and the United States were uneasy for another reason. The U.S. government wanted to buy California from Mexico. But the Mexican government refused to discuss selling California. In fact, Mexico cut off relations with the United States.

Texas created another source of tension between the United States and Mexico. The two nations disagreed about the border between Mexico and Texas. In 1846, the dispute led to the Mexican War between the United States and Mexico. U.S. forces captured California in early 1847. Later that year, an American army led by General Winfield Scott captured the Mexican capital of Mexico City.

After winning the war, the United States acquired about half of Mexico's territory in the Treaty of Guadalupe Hidalgo. The United States gained California and land that would make up all or part of the states of New Mexico, Utah, Nevada, Arizona, and Colorado.

Even during the war, people had migrated west. In the spring of 1846, more than 80 men, women, and children boarded wagons and left Illinois for California. Many of those in the wagon train were members of the Donner family. The group therefore became known as the Donner party.

By October, they had reached the towering Sierra Nevada in eastern California. Early snowfall forced them to stop for the winter.

Winfield Scott

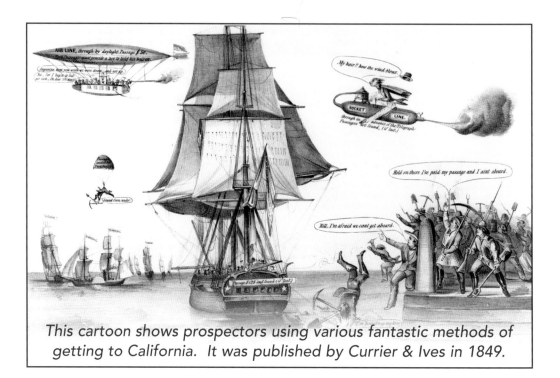

This cartoon shows prospectors using various fantastic methods of getting to California. It was published by Currier & Ives in 1849.

They set up camp but ran out of food. Rescuers managed to save 47 people. According to accounts at the time, some members of the Donner party resorted to cannibalism to survive.

News about the Donner party failed to discourage people from traveling west. In fact, more people moved west to settle. On January 24, 1848, an event occurred that attracted more Americans to California. A carpenter named James W. Marshall discovered gold in a fork of the American River in central California. Marshall's discovery set off the California gold rush. By 1849, thousands of people from all over the world had converged on California. Among those who journeyed to California were Chinese fortune hunters, who had heard rumors about a gold mountain.

People in the eastern United States faced difficult journeys to reach the goldfields. The Panama Canal did not exist yet, so sea voyages to California were long. One way to get to California was to sail around South America. This voyage could take as long as six months. Food and water stored this long often went bad on ships.

A shorter voyage took gold seekers to the Isthmus of Panama. At the isthmus, travelers crossed the narrow strip of land to catch another ship for California. However, this passage also had severe drawbacks. Travelers ran the risk of catching deadly diseases such as malaria and cholera. In addition, ships were not always available on the Pacific side of the isthmus to take people to California.

Another way for gold seekers to get to California was the overland route across the country. But this route presented its own dangers. Water sources along the route were often infected with cholera. Scarcity of water was another problem, especially in the desert of modern-day Nevada. The lack of water killed many oxen, mules, and horses that pulled wagons over the trail. Some gold seekers found themselves walking to California.

Thousands of people overcame the obstacles that made travel to California so miserable. In 1848, California's non-Native American population had been about 14,000. By 1850, it was more than 100,000. Enough people lived in California for the territory to be granted statehood. On September 9, 1850, California became the thirty-first state.

Settlers cross the Nevada desert on their way to California.

SUCCESS IN THE SIERRAS

The addition of California to the United States fueled serious discussions about a transcontinental railroad. On March 2, 1853, Congress passed the Pacific Railroad Survey Bill. The bill authorized Secretary of War Jefferson Davis to plan explorations of possible routes for a transcontinental railroad. Under Davis's orders, teams of soldiers searched for passages through mountain ranges in the West.

U.S. troops explored several possible routes. One team looked for a passage through the Cascade Mountains east of Puget Sound. Another party searched for a central route along the thirty-eighth parallel. The leader of this expedition, Lieutenant John W. Gunnison, was killed by Native Americans in the Utah Territory. A third group explored a route from Arkansas to Los Angeles, California. A later expedition searched for a route through Texas and present-day New Mexico and Arizona.

The army explored different regions because U.S. leaders supported different routes. U.S. Senator William H. Gwin of California favored a southern route. Washington Territory governor Isaac I. Stevens supported a northern railroad between the Washington and Minnesota territories.

Leaders also failed to agree upon a route because of slavery. In 1850, about 3 million blacks were enslaved in Southern states.

Jefferson Davis

There, slaves toiled on cotton plantations and performed other tasks. Northern states had abolished slavery. Northerners opposed a southern route for the transcontinental railroad. They feared this route would allow Southerners to spread their influence westward.

While political leaders argued about the route, another man dreamed of a transcontinental railroad. That person was Theodore Judah. He earned his great reputation by planning the Niagara Gorge railroad in the early 1850s. This railroad ran along the gorge from Niagara Falls to Lewiston, New York. It was considered an engineering wonder at the time.

Judah's skills as an engineer attracted the attention of Colonel Charles Lincoln Wilson. Wilson's company, Sacramento Valley Railroad, was planning the first railroad in California. He offered Judah a job, which the young engineer accepted. In 1854, Judah and his wife, Anna, sailed for California.

In California, Judah helped the company build a rail line from Sacramento to Folsom. But Judah was also obsessed with building a transcontinental railroad. He began to explore the Sierra Nevada. Judah then wrote a report called Practical Plan for Building the Pacific Railroad. The plan outlined a central route through the Great Plains that ended in the Sacramento Valley. In early 1857, Judah sent copies of his report to U.S. president James Buchanan and to members of Congress.

But Judah's reputation was suffering. His passion about a transcontinental railroad made some question Judah's sanity. A few people began to call him "Crazy" Judah.

Not everybody thought Judah was crazy. Some Californians supported a transcontinental railroad, and they urged the California legislature to back the project. On September 20, 1859, the legislature held a convention for a transcontinental railroad. Delegates from California, Oregon, and the territories of Washington and Arizona attended the convention. At the end of the convention, the delegates appointed Judah to appeal to Congress for a transcontinental railroad. In October, the Judahs left for Washington DC.

In the capital, Judah argued for a transcontinental railroad. But leaders were disturbed by the crisis over slavery. Many feared that the Southern states would leave the Union.

Judah asserted that a transcontinental railroad would help the country. The railroad would connect California to the rest of the country and secure the state's loyalty. Despite this argument, Judah failed to get greater congressional support for a transcontinental railroad. The Judahs returned to California.

In 1860, Judah's luck improved. His friend Daniel W. Strong invited Judah into the Sierra Nevada. Strong owned a store in the mining town of Dutch Flat. He knew the mountains well, and claimed to have found a passage through the Sierras.

Theodore Judah

The two men rode horses to the mountain pass where the Donner party had struggled to survive. Judah viewed the landscape and realized this was the solution. The pass avoided one of the most challenging aspects of the mountain range. The Sierra Nevada is made up of two parallel ridges. But this route did not cross the second ridge.

Judah and Strong moved quickly to capitalize on the discovery. They formed the Central Pacific Railroad Company. But they would need to raise thousands of dollars before the company could become a legal corporation. Judah believed he could easily find investors. After all, San Francisco and Sacramento were full of wealthy men who had taken risks during the gold rush. Judah, however, was disappointed. Few people were willing to invest in his railroad company.

Judah continued to seek investors. In November 1860, he spoke before a group at the St. Charles Hotel in Sacramento. Afterward, Collis Huntington invited

Collis Huntington

Mark Hopkins   *Leland Stanford*

Judah to talk further about the plan to build a railroad through the
Sierras. Huntington owned a hardware store and had become a
successful businessman during the gold rush. But he saw the railroad
as more than an investment. He believed the railroad would help
keep California in the Union.

Huntington and Judah met a couple of times. Then, Huntington
introduced the engineer to more men interested in Judah's plan.
These men were Mark Hopkins, Leland Stanford, and Charles Crocker.
Like Huntington, they were all businessmen. Hopkins was
Huntington's business partner. Stanford ran a grocery store, but he
was also active in politics. Crocker owned a dry-goods store.

The Central Pacific Railroad company is formed.

These men peppered Judah with questions. They soon agreed to purchase enough stock to allow the company to incorporate. In addition, they contributed money for Judah to survey in the Sierra Nevada. Huntington, Hopkins, Stanford, and Crocker helped make the Central Pacific Railroad a reality. They became known as "The Big Four" in the company.

Judah finished his survey in August 1861. By October, he had completed a report that included costs for building the rail line from Sacramento to the Nevada border. That same month, the company sent Judah back to Washington DC to gain congressional support for the railroad project. This time, Judah had better luck before he reached the capital. A fellow passenger was U.S. representative Aaron Sargent of California. On the long trip to Washington DC, Judah and Sargent discussed the Central Pacific Railroad's plans.

Meanwhile, political events benefited the proposed railroad. Stanford was elected governor of California. He was now in a better position to help building a railroad through the Sierras.

Another development also helped the railroad. Eleven Southern states broke away from the United States. These states formed the Confederate States of America in early 1861. The decision to leave the Union provoked the Civil War between Northern and Southern states. The war determined the route of the transcontinental railroad. If there were such a railroad, it would not have a southern route that involved the Confederate states.

Aaron Sargent

RAILROAD ACT

The war made a transcontinental railroad seem more important. Representative Sargent saw it that way. He was assigned to the House Pacific Railroad Committee. In January 1862, he gave a speech in Congress about a transcontinental railroad. He argued that such a railroad would bind California to the Union.

After the speech, Sargent worked on a bill in a railroad subcommittee. Judah was appointed the subcommittee's clerk. Later, Judah was named clerk of a House Select Committee on the Pacific Railroad. He also became clerk for the Senate Committee on Pacific Railroads. As clerk, Judah could greatly influence railroad legislation.

The bill enjoyed wide support in government. President Abraham Lincoln favored the bill, as did most members of Congress. In June, Congress voted on the Pacific Railroad Bill. It passed in the Senate 35 to 5, and in the House 104 to 21. Lincoln signed the bill on July 1. Once signed, the legislation became known as the Pacific Railway Act of 1862.

The act authorized Central Pacific Railroad to begin construction in Sacramento and proceed eastward. The act also created another company named the Union Pacific Railroad. This company

Abraham Lincoln

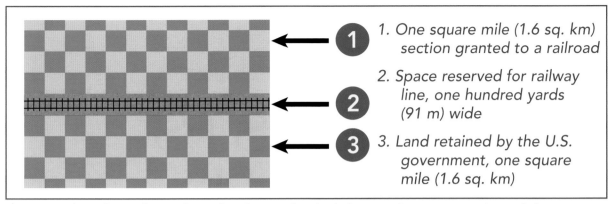

This chart shows how land was divided during the construction of the transcontinental railroad.

would start at the Missouri River and build track westward. The deadline for completing the railroad was July 1, 1876.

The Pacific Railway Act also transferred public land to the companies. Each company would receive 200 feet (61 m) of land on each side of the track. In addition, the government gave the companies alternating sections of land along the route. This land amounted to 6,400 acres (2,590 ha) per mile (1.6 km).

It looked like the federal government was giving a lot of land to the railroad companies. But the government was also retaining alternate sections of public land along the route. This government land would increase in value as the transcontinental railroad was built. Towns and farms would spring up along the route, increasing the price of the land.

The Pacific Railway Act also authorized the government to loan money to the railroad companies. This financial aid came in the form of government bonds. The companies would receive bonds of a certain value depending on the difficulty of construction. Companies would receive bonds of $16,000 for every mile (1.6 km) of construction in level areas. They would get bonds of $32,00 for every mile (1.6 km) of track in foothills. They would receive bonds of $48,000 for every mile (1.6 km) of track built in the mountains.

"HE RESTS FROM HIS LABORS"

Soon, relations between Judah and the Big Four began to fray. Judah was the chief engineer for the Central Pacific Railroad. He resented the questionable business practices of Huntington, Stanford, Hopkins, and Crocker.

One issue concerned the creation of Charles Crocker & Company. In December, Crocker formed this company to begin construction of the western part of the railroad. At the time, Crocker also served on the Central Pacific Railroad's board of directors. The Central Pacific Railroad would pay Crocker $400,000 to build the first 18 miles (29 km) of track. Crocker resigned from the board to avoid a conflict of interest. However, Crocker was replaced on the board by his brother Edwin.

Judah was agitated. He distrusted Crocker, who had never supervised a construction project. Also, Judah feared that the Big Four would use Charles Crocker & Company to became rich at the expense of the railroad.

Construction of the western part of the transcontinental railroad officially began on January 8, 1863. The groundbreaking was held in

K Street in Sacramento, California, in the early 1860s

the muddy streets of Sacramento. Governor Stanford and Crocker gave speeches, but their colleagues were absent. Hopkins was worried about the project's finances and did not attend. Judah was in the Sierras. Huntington was on the East Coast promoting the railroad.

During the groundbreaking, Stanford overturned a scoop of soil with a silver-bladed spade. Meanwhile, a steam pile driver did the real work along the American River. The machine was one of the few pieces of modern technology used for construction.

Later, Judah and the Big Four grew more divided. Judah continued to object to the Big Four's business dealings. For example, Stanford used his position as governor to acquire $1 million in state money for the Central Pacific Railroad.

There were other improper business practices. The Pacific Railway Act said that President Lincoln would determine the boundary of the Sierra Nevada. But Lincoln was on the other side of the country and would need to rely on others for information about the boundary. Determining the boundary was important. The Central Pacific Railroad would receive more in government bonds for construction in the mountains.

Governor Stanford sent state geologist Josiah Whitney and Crocker to determine the western boundary of the Sierra Nevada. They claimed that the mountains began near Arcade Creek. This location was 15 miles (24 km) farther west than where the mountains really began. However, beginning the Sierras at the Arcade Creek location allowed the Central Pacific Railroad to receive an additional $480,000 in government bonds. Judah was shocked. He had explored the Sierra Nevada, and knew the range's true western boundary.

The dispute between Judah and the Big Four reached a critical point. Judah wanted to regain control of the company he had started. On October 3, 1863, the Judahs sailed from California. Their journey took them across the Isthmus of Panama. Judah planned to travel to the East Coast to raise money. He hoped to use this money to buy back control of the Central Pacific Railroad.

During the journey, Judah became sick. He probably had yellow fever. On October 26, Judah's ship arrived in New York City. He was taken to a hotel where Anna and a doctor cared for him. Judah died on November 2. Anna Judah buried her husband in Greenfield, Massachusetts. The inscription on his headstone reads, "He rests from his labors."

The Sierra Nevada

CORRUPTION AND HONEST WORK

Theodore Judah was gone. But the hard work of planning the transcontinental railroad continued. On November 17, 1863, President Lincoln selected the eastern point of the transcontinental railroad. He chose the Omaha and Council Bluffs area along the Missouri River.

Thomas Durant decided to start the railroad in Omaha in the Nebraska Territory. Durant was vice president and general manager of the Union Pacific Railroad. He also owned property in Omaha. Starting the railroad in Omaha would make his land more valuable. The Omaha location had another advantage for Durant. The Union Pacific Railroad would not have to pay to build a bridge over the Missouri River.

A groundbreaking ceremony took place in Omaha on December 2. Politicians and Union Pacific officials gave speeches. But almost no actual construction took place. The Union Pacific was short of money, labor, and supplies.

Durant set about improving the Union Pacific's financial situation. He went to Washington DC, where he sought to gain more government support for his railroad. Meanwhile, Huntington was

Peter Dey

Thomas Durant

also in Washington DC. Both men bribed members of Congress to receive government help.

Durant's and Huntington's efforts paid off with the passage of the Pacific Railway Act of 1864. The act increased the amount of money the government would loan to the railroad companies. In addition, it increased the amount of land the companies would receive along the railroad tracks. Instead of 6,400 acres (2,590 ha) per mile, the companies would get 12,800 acres (5,180 ha).

Durant was not finished scheming. In 1864, Durant and other business partners created a company called Crédit Mobilier. They used the company to profit from railroad construction.

The deceit worked this way. Crédit Moblier submitted the only bid to the Union Pacific for construction. This bid was accepted. But Crédit Mobilier inflated its cost estimates for construction. The company then hired other companies to do the actual work. Durant and others pocketed the extra money. The Union Pacific's chief engineer, Peter Dey, was disgusted with this dishonesty. He resigned from the company.

While men such as Durant and Huntington plotted and made money, gangs of workers built the railroad. At first, the lack of workers hindered progress. The Civil War drained much of the nation's labor force. By 1865, only 40 miles (64 km) of track had been laid outside of Omaha. That same year, the Union defeated Confederate forces, ending the war. Plenty of army veterans were now available to work on the railroad.

The scale of the construction, however, required even more workers. Consequently, both the Union Pacific and Central Pacific relied on immigrants for labor. The Union Pacific brought in Irish immigrants, who had been living in eastern U.S. cities. The Central Pacific depended on thousands of Chinese immigrants. By 1868, about 12,000 Chinese worked for the Central Pacific. Although most of the company's workers were Chinese, Irish immigrants also worked on the western section of the railroad.

Workers for the Central Pacific Railroad confronted a formidable task. They had to blast and drill tunnels through the granite of the Sierra Nevada. Crews used blasting powder to clear away rock. Still, the work was extremely slow.

To speed up progress, the railroad company tried a different tactic. Chinese workers in baskets were lowered along the sides of cliffs. The workers drilled holes into the cliffs and packed the holes with explosives. They lit fuses to the explosives and then were pulled back up. The job was dangerous. Sometimes workers were killed by explosions or hit by flying rocks.

Crews faced another challenge. They worked during the Sierra Nevada's brutal winters. One engineer counted more than 40 snowstorms during the winter of 1866–1867. The abundance of

PACIFIC RAILWAY LINES

CANADA

Seattle
Tacoma
WA

Great Northern (1893)

OR

MT

ND

Duluth

ID

North Pacific (1883)

MN

WI

CA

Central Pacific (1869)

Junction 1869

WY

SD

Ogden

NV

UT

San Francisco

CO

NE

Omaha

IA

Union Pacific (1869)

KS

Atchison

Topeka

IL

MO

os Angeles

AZ

Atchison, Topeka and Santa Fe (1884)

NM

OK

AR

MS

TX

LA

New Orleans

Southern Pacific (1884)

Pacific
Ocean

N

MEXICO

Gulf of Mexico

This map shows various
transcontinental lines and when they
were completed.

snow created avalanches, which swept down the mountains and buried crews. The Central Pacific Railroad lost many workers to avalanches. The company also built roofs over some track to keep the path clear of snow.

By 1867, crews began working on the Summit Tunnel. Engineers estimated that the tunnel would be 1,659 feet (506 m) long. At the current rate of progress, it would take 15 months to finish the tunnel. This was too much time. Charles and Edwin Crocker decided the company needed to try an explosive called nitroglycerin.

In the 1860s, nitroglycerin was a new invention. The Swedish inventor Alfred Nobel used nitroglycerin to make dynamite. However, the Central Pacific Railroad did not use dynamite. Instead, crews worked with the pure, more dangerous nitroglycerin. The company hired British chemist James Howden to produce nitroglycerin in the mountains. This reduced the danger of transporting such a hazardous material over a great distance.

Nitroglycerin was several times more powerful than blasting powder. This new explosive allowed crews to blast away more rock at a faster rate. By November 1867, the tunnel was cleared and track was laid through it. A train chugged through the structure to celebrate the Summit Tunnel's completion. Although nitroglycerin aided construction, the Central Pacific Railroad did not use the explosive again.

The Union Pacific crews did not have to contend with the Sierra Nevada. They worked mostly in the flatter area of the Great Plains. But they did have to cope with the hostility of Native Americans. The 1860s were a time of violence between whites and Native Americans on the plains. In November 1864, U.S. forces massacred about 150 Cheyenne Native Americans near Sand Creek in the

Alfred Nobel

Colorado Territory. Also, white settlers migrated through Native American land on their way to goldfields in present-day Montana. The U.S. Army also built forts along the trail.

Native Americans also resented the transcontinental railroad, which would bring more whites west. Warriors from the Lakota, Cheyenne, and Arapaho tribes struck against the railroad. They attacked surveyors and construction crews. They also tore up track and derailed trains. The military experience of some of the railroad workers helped them. In 1866, a crew drove off Native Americans who had attacked a train near Plum Creek in the Nebraska Territory.

The most effective way to address these attacks was to hire other Native Americans to fight. The Pawnee, a longtime enemy of the Lakota, served as scouts in the U.S. Army. Pawnee scouts fought against the other Plains Native Americans. They also protected

Cheyenne Native Americans attack a Union Pacific work crew.

railroad surveyors and crews. The Pawnee could not stop all the attacks, but they were good soldiers. One general praised the Pawnee for the services they provided.

Life for railroad workers was filled with danger and hard work. When they didn't work, they often engaged in the wild pastimes of the frontier. This was especially true of workers for the Union Pacific Railroad. Saloons and gambling houses sprang up near the crews and followed them west. This traveling camp of wildness was known as "Hell on Wheels." A newspaper editor who saw one of these outposts gave them that name.

Chinese workers were more restrained in their behavior. For one thing, they tended to avoid alcohol and drank tea instead. Because they made their tea with boiled water, Chinese workers did not suffer from the dysentery that afflicted other laborers.

A CONTINENT CONNECTED

The Union Pacific and Central Pacific faced stiff challenges when building the railroad. But they were also encouraged to build tracks as fast as possible. The companies received more land and more government bonds for each mile of track they built. This arrangement set off a furious race between the two railroad companies.

Union Pacific crews built track at an impressive rate. In October 1868, crews built about 8 miles (13 km) of track in one day. Durant contacted Charles Crocker. Durant bet $10,000 that the Union Pacific's record could not be broken. Crocker accepted the bet.

On April 28, 1869, Crocker prepared to surpass the record in northern Utah. About 5,000 workers participated in the massive undertaking. Irish and Chinese workers hustled all day to lay track. Each worker had a specific task. Some carried rails or railroad ties. Others hammered spikes. They shattered the record by building 10 miles (16 km) of track by the end of the day.

The Union Pacific did not have a chance to beat the record. Its crews were within 9 miles (14.5 km) of the meeting point at Promontory Summit. Immigrants and American workers finished the transcontinental railroad in May 1869. It is unknown whether Durant ever paid the bet to Crocker.

Marker commemorating the record-breaking 10 miles (16 km) of track laid in one day

A group of hunters disembarks from a train to shoot buffalo.

The nation celebrated the track's completion. But Native Americans detested the transcontinental railroad. The railroad ran through the homeland of the Plains Native Americans. More white settlers followed the rails west. As more whites moved to the plains, the U.S. government continued placing Native Americans on reservations. By 1890, Native Americans had lost even the hunting grounds that had been promised them.

The expansion of the railroad also led to the near extinction of the buffalo. Native Americans on the plains depended on the buffalo for food. The railroad brought white hunters to the plains who then slaughtered the buffalo. Buffalo hides were then shipped by rail to manufacturers in the east. Once, millions of buffalo roamed the plains. By 1880, only 1,000 buffalo were left.

While Native Americans suffered because of the railroad, most of the country benefited. The transcontinental railroad made it cheaper to ship goods around the country. Lower shipping costs meant that a truly continental economy could develop in the United States. Goods from the East Coast could now be easily transported to the West Coast. This sparked a production boom. By 1880, the transcontinental railroad was moving $50 million of freight every year.

The transcontinental railroad spurred transportation in the United States. It gave people a faster way to travel between the coasts. Before the transcontinental railroad, people had to travel for months to reach the other side of the country. The transcontinental railroad allowed people to travel from New York City to San Francisco in a week.

The transcontinental railroad brought both harm and benefits to people living in the United States. But undoubtedly the railroad altered the nation. The transcontinental railroad was one of the greatest engineering feats in the nineteenth century.

Central Pacific workers lay track.

Workers for the Central Pacific and Union Pacific railroads celebrate the completion of the transcontinental railroad at Promontory Summit. A train from each company faces each other on the finished line and workers toast each other and shake hands.

Stanford and Durant also shook hands after the final spike was driven. Durant then said, "There is henceforth but one Pacific Railroad in the United States."

Shortly after, lawlessness prevailed, and souvenir hunters began looking for the commemorative spikes. They also chipped away pieces of railroad ties and rails. The commemorative spikes, however, had already been removed to a safer location.

TIMELINE

1830 William Redfield suggests building a railroad line from the Atlantic coast to the Mississippi River valley.

1853 On March 2, Congress passes the Pacific Railroad Survey Bill.

1857 Theodore Judah sends copies of his Practical Plan for Building the Pacific Railroad to U.S. president James Buchanan and to members of Congress.

1859 On September 20, California hosts a convention about building a transcontinental railroad. Judah is elected to urge Congress to support the railroad project.

1860 Daniel W. Strong and Judah discover a route through the Sierra Nevada for the transcontinental railroad. They soon found the Central Pacific Railroad Company.

Collis Huntington, Mark Hopkins, Leland Stanford, and Charles Crocker agree to back the Central Pacific Railroad Company. They become known as "The Big Four."

1861 to 1865 The Civil War is fought between the United States of America and the Confederate States of America. The United States wins, preserving the Union.

1862 The Pacific Railway Act of 1862 is passed, authorizing the building of a transcontinental railroad. It also creates the Union Pacific Railroad company to build part of the railroad.

1863	On January 8, the Central Pacific begins work on the western part of the transcontinental railroad near Sacramento, California.
	On December 2, the Union Pacific begins work on its portion of the transcontinental railroad.
1864	The Pacific Railway Act of 1864 is passed, increasing the reward each railroad company received for laying track.
1867	The Central Pacific begins work on the Summit Tunnel through the Sierra Nevada.
	Because of slow progress on the Summit Tunnel, the Central Pacific hires James Howden to produce nitroglycerin to speed blasting.
1868	In October, the Union Pacific lays 8 miles (13 km) of track in one day. Durant bets Crocker that the Central Pacific cannot beat this record.
1869	On April 28, the Central Pacific beats the Union Pacific's record by laying 10 miles (16 km) of track in one day.
	On May 10, the nation celebrates the completion of the transcontinental railroad.

American Moments

FAST FACTS

At the time of the transcontinental railroad, Chinese immigrants were often called "celestials." This is because China was then known as the "Celestial Kingdom."

The Central Pacific Railroad Company made a "treaty" with the Paiute Native Americans. This would allow the Paiute to ride trains for free for not making trouble for the transcontinental railroad. Passengers later complained about riding with Native Americans. Paiute chiefs were then forced to ride in baggage cars or to hang onto the side of the train when they traveled by rail.

Native American men and women were also recruited to work on the Central Pacific Railroad. One observer noticed the women working and was shocked to find that they handled the tools well. He noted that "they out-did the men."

As the Union Pacific Railroad completed its part of the transcontinental track, settlers and shopkeepers sometimes took over railroad land without paying. Some Union Pacific agents were even threatened with death if they tried to force the squatters to pay in Cheyenne, Wyoming. Periodically, U.S. troops were called to clear these ruffians out.

Four other transcontinental rail lines were built before the end of the nineteenth century. They were the Southern Pacific, Northern Pacific, Great Northern, and the Atchison, Topeka, and Santa Fe lines. The Atchison, Topeka, and Santa Fe line extended from California to Missouri. The Northern Pacific and Great Northern lines connected Washington and Minnesota. New Orleans, Louisiana, and Los Angeles, California, were connected by the Southern Pacific line.

Leland Stanford went on to found Stanford University on his estate in Palo Alto, California, in 1891. It was founded in memory of Stanford's son, Leland Stanford Jr. Young Leland died at the age of 15 of typhoid fever. The day after his son's death, Stanford told his wife, "The children of California shall be our children."

WEB SITES
WWW.ABDOPUB.COM

Would you like to learn more about the transcontinental railroad? Please visit **www.abdopub.com** to find up-to-date Web site links about the transcontinental railroad and other American moments. These links are routinely monitored and updated to provide the most current information available.

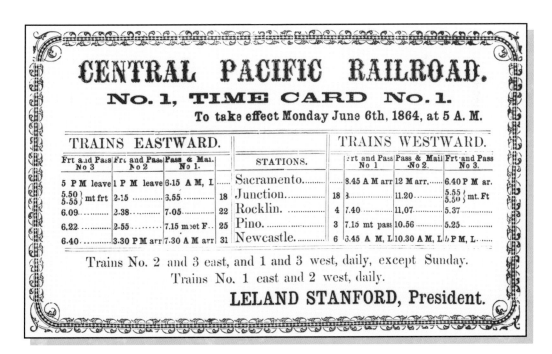

Timetable for the Central Pacific Railroad

GLOSSARY

annex: to add land to a nation.

apparatus: equipment designed for a specific purpose.

bond: a certificate sold by a government. The certificate promises to pay its purchase price plus interest at a given future date.

cholera: a disease of the intestines that includes severe vomiting and diarrhea.

dysentery: a disease that causes severe diarrhea.

foothills: a hilly region at the base of a mountain range.

gorge: a deep, narrow passage between steep, rocky walls or mountains.

incorporate: to form into a legal corporation.

isthmus: a narrow strip of land connecting two larger areas.

malaria: a disease spread by mosquitoes that causes chills and fever.

Panama Canal: a narrow canal across Panama that connects the Atlantic and Pacific Oceans.

pile driver: a machine that drives concrete, timber, or steel into the ground.

sanction: to officially approve.

switchback: a section of road or railroad that zigzags to aid an uphill climb.

technology: the use of scientific knowledge to solve practical problems.

telegraph: a system of communication made of wires in which messages are transmitted electronically.

terrain: the physical features of an area of land. Mountains, rivers, and canyons can all be part of a terrain.

transcontinental: crossing a continent.

yellow fever: a tropical disease transmitted by mosquitoes. Symptoms include headache, backache, fever, nausea, and vomiting. If patients do not recover, they can die within six to seven days of experiencing symptoms.

INDEX